Workplace Diversity

— How to Get It Right

By
Sylvio (Syd) A. Gravel, M.O.M.
Police Staff Sergeant (ret'd)

Budd Publishing/Syd A. Gravel
Ottawa, Ontario

Published by: Budd Publishing/Syd A. Gravel

URL: http://www.56secondsbook.com

Library and Archives Canada Cataloguing in Publication

Gravel, Sylvio A., 1952-, author

   Workplace diversity— how to get it right / Sylvio A. Gravel.

Issued in print and electronic formats.

ISBN 978-0-9881316-2-0 (pbk.).—ISBN 978-0-9881316-3-7 (pdf)

   1. Diversity in the workplace. I. Title.

HF5549.5.M5G73 2014   658.3008   C2014-902637-4
      C2014-902638-2

Cover illustration: www.istockphoto.com

Cover and Book Design: Budd Publishing

Editor: Eleanor Sawyer

PRINTED IN U.S.A.

To my grandchildren.

*Leave the campsite in a better
condition than when you arrived.*

Grandpa did this!

Contents

Contents

Acknowledgements

Change management projects don't happen on the back of one person's work or commitment. There were many people involved in this project in order for it to succeed. I would like to acknowledge, in particular, Peggy Kampouris, Trevor Wilson, Chief Vince Bevan, Deputy Chief Larry Hill, Debra Frazer, Christine Roy, Paul Gallant, Joanne Doré, Onalee Wyman, Margaret MacDonald, Carl Nicholson, Trish Ferguson, David Pepper, Nathalya Kuziak, Dr. Carina Fiedeldey-Van Dijk and Dr. Linda Duxbury.

There were also many members of the community on the Community and Police Action Committee (COMPAC) and on the advisory committee who helped each and every step of the way, as well as many members of the Ottawa Police Service who participated in managing the change process.

I also want to say a very special thank you to my wife, Judy, who never doubted my ability to work through anything.

Introduction

Not every organization or business, whether private or public, has the management skills or the human resources to successfully create a more diverse workplace. I was fortunate to have this experience while working for the Ottawa Police Service, which had a human resources division of more than ten staff. I also had a recruiting and training team.

My wife, on the other hand, is the owner of a small business with one full-time seasonal staff and four part-time seasonal staff. She is the chief executive officer (CEO), chief operating officer (COO), president, chair of the board, owner, manager, sales clerk, cook, bookkeeper, bottle washer and facility maintenance engineer all in one. She has to manage every project for her business.

Many small organizations and businesses don't have the luxury of a human resources department or manager. This is why I wrote this book. I want to give organizations and individuals the information they will need to develop and implement a diversity project in their workplace. Doing this will help their businesses and organizations grow and thrive without the costs of hiring and developing a human resources infrastructure.

This book details the step-by-step process of one organization's transformation through a workplace diversity project and the interesting lessons that were learned. What is most interesting about this story is that it is about an organization that was entrenched—and still is—in 150 years or more of paramilitary traditions. Yet the Ottawa Police Service still managed to make its way through a very complex social change and did so very successfully.

The book describes how a community of very frustrated people willingly volunteered—both inside and outside the organization—to help in the transition. It was a question of asking for their help and the book will provide information on how to do this. The book also looks at the issues around diversity: what it means to different people, how including more diversity in the workplace enriches the organization, and how to offer people a venue to express their concerns, thoughts and ideas.

Although my experience is based on my work with the Ottawa Police Service, in *Workplace Diversity—How to Get It Right*, I will share all the crucial lessons and tips I learned to help organizations and small businesses to develop a diversity project and to implement it in the workplace as simply and as effectively as possible.

From Panicked

In 2002, I was a sergeant assigned to training with the Ottawa Police Service in Ontario, Canada. I was asked to take over the staff sergeant position in human resources for a short three-month stint to cover for the incumbent staff sergeant who was on special leave.

I don't know how it works in your world but, in my world, when you are sitting in someone else's management chair for a short period of time, you basically just want to babysit the position. You don't want to initiate anything new. You hope you don't have to make any changes to the status quo and you pray that nothing becomes a problem, so that the person, who really owns the position, has to come back to a mess that you couldn't fix in the time you were there.

I arrived in human resources to find that a class of thirty recruits had just gone through the entire hiring process. My job at this stage was to organize the welcoming ceremony for them. No big deal and easy to do! However, the chief wanted to show off our latest recruits in a public event rather than in an internal ceremony. He invited many community leaders to attend, which meant that the ceremony was now going to be held at a large convention centre. It would also attract some local media attention.

When the new recruits were paraded up on stage to receive their badges and welcomed to the police service, what became evident was the disconnect between what the class looked like versus what the community leaders looked like. Not only was there no reflection of the diversity among the invited guests, there didn't appear to be any connection between our recruits and the community leaders either.

In a very short number of years, the City of Ottawa had developed a very diverse community, which represented over sixty different ethnic cultures speaking over seventy-two different languages. The Ottawa Police Service certainly hadn't shifted as quickly or as diversely. Our class of recruits had maintained the status quo of white males and the diversity factors were limited to education, socioeconomic background, age and a narrow view about gender.

We really didn't even know how much diversity we had within our organization because, unlike the community which had measured itself against the federal government's census, we had never measured ourselves within the organization. We really didn't know for sure what communities and cultures we were connected to when it came to diversity, or how wide the range of secondary dimensions, that is, those we could not see in people, was in the organization. Our primary dimensions—those we could see—were certainly not very diverse, considering what we were seeing within the community.

Community leaders certainly expressed their concerns to the chief with regard to how disconnected we appeared to be in terms of reflecting the community and its diversity. There was no mistaking the tone and the message from the community. Those sentiments filtered down to me.

For years, many community leaders had worked hard, and quietly in the background, to try and effect change within the police service, knowing full well that, unless some effort was made to create inclusivity and diversity, the organization would fall behind in its efforts and even in its ability to protect the community as a whole as the service was mandated to do.

Although ongoing efforts were acknowledged, very little had changed within the organization. The effort required more than an attempt to appease; it required an effort to change not only recruiting and frontline services but also how we managed our people and presented ourselves as an organization top down.

In four months, we would be hiring another class of recruits and it was made clear to me that I had better make certain that the new recruits reflected the community and would connect well with it. It was a reasonable request, considering the circumstances, but it put me in panic mode. I knew the traditions within the service: more of the same old-same old and don't rock the boat.

With over nine hundred applications on file, I thought this would be an easy fix. The next day, I asked my staff to review all the applications and identify those that appeared to reflect the diversity of the community in any and all aspects. A few days later, staff gave me a small number of files but not enough to create a significant change from our traditional hiring practices. I was disappointed and I realized that this was going to require more than just pulling files out of the application cabinet.

I then called on a few of our own visible minority officers to ask them to assist me in reaching out to their various communities. This was the beginning of the revelation stage for me about how other people within the organization truly saw it. I had forgotten how difficult it was to be different in the organization. Many of these officers pointed out to me that not everything was sunny and rosy in the Ottawa Police

Service. I had known at one time about these difficulties on a personal level but had forgotten.

As a young recruit, I was the target of many demeaning jokes that related to the fact that I was a French-Canadian. Every time I made a mistake in the learning process it was because I was French. If others made the same mistake, it was because they were learning. However, over time, the bigots within the organization found other targets and eventually my being French faded away. I became one of the "boys" and, as a white male, I eventually came to live a fairly sheltered life within the police organization.

Many of these minority officers whom I was now speaking with were truly struggling with the idea of staying in the service. The idea of encouraging others within their communities to join us was not something that appealed to them. So, with almost no files in the applicant filing cabinet to draw from, and my fellow officers not exactly excited about getting involved in recruiting applicants, I decided to reach out to the various community leaders.

When I asked many of them to help us reach out to young people in their communities, who might be interested in policing as a career, they were interested and willing to help. But they wanted to know how willing and serious the Ottawa Police Service was in its commitment to support their community efforts and involvement in the recruitment process. These community leaders also wanted to ensure that I was not simply putting in an effort at the front end of recruiting and welcoming new recruits into a poisoned environment, which would lead them to seek a way out shortly after being hired. I couldn't give them any assurances at this point.

I was now starting to panic, even more so, because I had three months left to hire the next class. What I thought would be an easy fix was not turning out that way.

It got worse!

There was a changing of the guard occurring within the police service such as never seen before in its entire 150-year history. In the next five years, starting in 2002, we would see almost thirty percent of all senior officers potentially retire, with twenty percent of middle managers retiring as well. This would mean that over fifty percent of all these positions would be new to most officers. But the most shocking news was that over sixty percent of all frontline officers would have less than five years' experience within a couple of years, so we couldn't afford to lose anyone with experience.

We needed to hire almost one hundred officers per year, over the next five years, starting immediately under my interim watch as the commanding officer for recruiting. With three classes of recruits per year, this meant that thirty to thirty-five officers had to be hired every four months for five years. With a best practices ratio of twenty applications equaling one recruit, we needed two thousand applications on hand per year; we were starting with only nine hundred on file.

I was quickly discovering that just about every other police service was running into the same problem. Organizations such as the Ontario Provincial Police, the Toronto Police and the RCMP were also hiring large numbers. In some cases, they needed more recruits than they were even equipped to train. And many of us were upset that officers, who joined as recruits within our organizations, were gaining a few years' experience and then quitting to join other organizations closer to their homes.

To make matters worse for me, the incumbent staff sergeant, whose position I was filling, decided to tender his retirement papers. Although I was on the promotional list, I wasn't next in line on that list, so the organization couldn't even give me the job I was temporarily doing even if they had wanted to. They had to appoint someone else—and they did. However, this staff sergeant was already on temporary assignment to another organization, so I was once again sitting in a position belonging to someone else, someone who was even less familiar with the job than me with my one month's experience. Not exactly the type of situation that encouraged a whole lot of faith in my ability to get this job done—me included!

I was now facing a whole slew of problems that just couldn't be ignored. I walked into the director's office and explained my concerns in relation to how complicated I thought the entire situation was. Within a few days, we met again but, this time, some senior officers were involved. Everyone from deputy chiefs and the director general to the directors of human resources, communications, community development and corporate planning was there. As acting staff sergeant, I was the lowest ranked officer (or civilian) in attendance. (Civilian directors are considered to have the rank equivalency of inspector.)

During the meeting, I shared what I thought the dilemma was that the organization was facing. Members discussed how best to address the problem. Whatever decision was made, I hoped that an inspector (someone not only with personal but also with positional power) would be appointed to carry on.

This is what my list of issues looked like:

1. Even though we had over nine hundred applications on file, with one hundred coming in every month, we needed two thousand applications on file as a starting point. Out of the nine hundred we had, very few reflected the diversity of our community. We needed to start a campaign to interest people in applying for jobs in the police service.

2. We had strong indications from our own members that our organization was not an attractive place to work at. We needed to find out why and address these issues.

3. We had community leaders and organizations willing to help us recruit in any way they could but they wanted to know how committed we were to supporting their efforts.

4. We had a massive wave of retirements coming. We needed to manage these numbers and attract people who would stay longer.

5. The window of opportunity to hire such large and diversified numbers of people was very short (considering point 4). We needed a plan with goals and timelines for a team to implement; we also needed a committed team.

6. We had a low-ranking officer (me) in charge of recruiting at a time when we needed someone with at least the rank of inspector to take charge and get things moving. There was no doubt that resources, including a budget, would have to be invested in this project. (I knew we would have to borrow from others within the organization and that the rank of staff sergeant was not a powerful enough position to allow discussions to occur at the higher ranks of noncommissioned officers [NCOs].)

Interestingly enough, while I saw a whole series of problems, the members at the meeting came to the conclusion that this was an opportunity to create change. They saw it as an opportunity to build a business case. When an organization is about to change fundamentally how it operates, there can be anxiety, stress, uneasiness and worry in the current workplace. It takes a sustained commitment of time and effort by the entire business or organization to address these changes. This is why it is important to have a business case. Fundamentally, a business case is a strategic plan that takes advantage of an opportunity to create change and there is a flow to how a business case rolls out, which I touch on in "Lesson 9."

The police service decided to call the business case the Outreach Recruitment Project. We discovered later that this was not a good name for the project as it led everyone in the organization to believe that the project was focused only on recruitment and not on overall management change. With everything that staff members had to concern themselves with on a day-to-day basis, taking on more work was not very attractive. When they learned about a new project called Outreach Recruitment, many were relieved, thinking that the project had nothing to do with them. We ended up spending a lot of time explaining how, in spite of the name of the project, the issues were not just about recruitment and that everyone had to get involved. I was relieved that the executive had taken the position that this was an opportunity to develop a business case to create change and had taken ownership of the project.

The first stage was to establish the case for change and to define clearly the need for it. In order to do this, senior management wanted to undertake various types of research to validate this opportunity. Although I was pleased with this approach, I was worried that starting a research process now would not make any difference for the next one or two classes of recruits. In the short term, the business case format did not lessen my worries. In the meantime, I focused on working with what I had on hand, while I waited for senior management to appoint the project manager so that I could get the help I needed. Later on, the director of human resources came to my office to advise that the person who was going to be responsible for the project had been selected.

It wasn't an inspector, whom I thought was required. It was me—a sergeant—at the bottom end of the management hierarchy.

Not one to back down from a challenge, I accepted my role.

To Passionate

We now went from a recruiting project to a complete management change project.

I was now assigned full-time to manage the project. I was assigned a civilian assistant and I continued to be an acting staff sergeant. A new confirmed staff sergeant was brought in to manage the recruiting side of the office. Along with me, a project management consultant started the complex process of developing a project charter with all its associated tools.

I found the introduction to the development of a formal project management process rather daunting—and tedious. I have strong personality traits—direct and dominating yet calculating—that tend toward detail and veer more strongly to just getting things done—a bit like a bull who can do a lot of damage in a fine-china shop. I drive toward the end product or goal.

The consultant, on the other hand, was detail-oriented as well but also more soft-spoken, people-oriented, patient and willing to compromise. This person was very caring, personable, ready and eager to please. I like people to get along too. But, if it's a choice between getting along and getting the job done, I have a tendency to go with getting the job done. The consultant also focused on getting the job done and did so very well. But she would do this by patiently reformatting the questions for those involved until she got the answers she needed, whereas I would rather do it myself than get into working things out with someone. Besides, I was panicking about how long all this was going to take to get started and to get some results.

I wasn't the most patient, understanding or flexible person for the consultant to work with. I made her job difficult as a result. Taking me through the step-by-step process of developing the plan for the formal project process was painful for me and tried her patience as well. Yet I thank her every day since then for the fact that she had such patience to take me to the end of the project.

Here is why.

The project charter outlined the following details:

- the purpose, goals and objectives;

- the critical success factors;

- the strategy;

- the interim and end products;

- the scope of and schedule for the project;

- the budget and constraints;

- the planning assumptions;

- a risk assessment;

- the organizational impacts;

- the reporting relationships;

- the project's priority status in the organization,

- sponsor responsibilities; and

- the completion criteria.

Best of all, the project charter approvals process took pressure off me. There was such clarity about what I had to do that I simply followed the map. When I saw all the signatures from those involved at the executive level, who supported the project charter, I realized that I was not going to be alone in implementing the project and its end products.

The reporting assignment matrix, known as RAM, was the next tool introduced to me and I absolutely came to love it. No matter what part of the project we started, we always decided first who had to approve each stage of the work. The lower the chain of command at the reporting level, the faster the work got done. The higher up the chain of command at the reporting level, the more likelihood of a delay. When challenged as to why there was a delay, I could usually point to an approval issue as a result of someone higher up in the chain of command who just couldn't find the time to do their part.

The to-do and the schedule tools were dreams come true in terms of managing who was doing what, how their work affected others and when things should be done. Every Monday morning, I would review the to-do lists and the schedule to see what was expected to be accomplished that week, by whom and who else would be affected if the work was either completed or late. What was on those lists helped me to plan my week.

As the project proceeded, the project management tools, designed by the consultant and handed over to me to work with, gave me a sense of comfort and control that I needed. I became more confident and passionate about both the process and the project itself.

To Success

The Outreach Recruitment Project was initially intended to deliver final results within three months at best and six months at worst. The overall project of managing organizational change in the police service, with a goal of becoming as diverse as our community, lasted over six years. Throughout those years, there were phenomenal numbers of small—yet very impactful and successful—changes that occurred at the time much to the benefit of the Ottawa Police Service and the community.

The following lists some of the changes that propelled the Ottawa Police Service (OPS) to be recognized as one of the most progressive and diverse police services in North America, all of which came out of the initial work from this project.

1. An internal research project that included both members of the community and police staff working together to come up with seventeen recommendations for change.

2. The formation of a diversity and recruitment advisory committee consisting of representation from within the community and from all staff levels internally.

3. A research document, developed by Carleton University for our executives, about managing the change that would be occurring in the organization.

4. The formation of an award-winning champion program for recruitment, with the community as a partner and with training for both community and OPS members together.

5. The formation of a Workplace Harassment Prevention Project to establish processes and a framework to support supervisory accountability that would address inappropriate employee behaviour with respect to workplace harassment and discrimination, and to create a respectful workplace.

6. The development of a Mediation Pilot Project, in partnership with the Centre for Conflict Education and Research, Carleton University.

7. A first-in-policing census to measure the assets we had in our human resources.

8. An English as a Second Language Program for new immigrants, with a focus on policing in

Ottawa, in partnership with the Ontario Provincial Police.

9. Every year after the first year of the project, each and every recruit class to include representation of approximately forty-five percent from visible minorities, females, Aboriginals and GLBTTQ members.

As a result of this work, the Ottawa Police Service received the following awards and accolades:

- The Ottawa Police Service was the first in Canada to be recognized by the Toronto Immigration Employment Centre for its recruiting practices.

- For its overall work, the Ottawa Police Service was acknowledged as an Innovator in Diversity Programs, by *Profiles in Diversity*, at the International Awards in 2006 in Cleveland, Ohio.

- The service was shortlisted as Employer of Choice in *Maclean's Magazine* in 2006 for Top 100 Best Employers.

- The service received the 2007 Civil Rights Award for the Champion Recruitment Program from the International Association of Chiefs of Police in New Orleans.

- For its overall successes, the Ottawa Police Service was acknowledged as an Innovator in Diversity

Programs, in *Profiles in Diversity*, at the
International Awards in 2008, in Cleveland, Ohio.

At the end of all this work, there were twelve key lessons
that I believe were crucial to our success. I share these
with you in the following chapters.

Lesson 1

ESTABLISH THE NEED FOR WORKPLACE DIVERSITY

Before moving forward with any workplace diversity plan, it is necessary to discuss why it's important to the organization, your staff and your community.

In our case, the community of diverse leaders had been working for years to try to persuade the Ottawa, Nepean and Gloucester Police Services to look at inclusivity and diversity as value-added to their organizations. The commitment had been minimal and based on the personal decision of each chief as they managed their services. However, once all these services were amalgamated into one organization in 2000 as the Ottawa Police Service, there was an opportunity as never before. While it is important to take advantage of an opportunity, there has to be a reason to do so.

To substantiate those reasons, we did some worldwide best practices research to see what other police services knew. The best examples came from other Canadian services such as those in Toronto, Calgary, Edmonton, Vancouver, Montreal and Sudbury. They had all done some very good work, so we connected with all of them for ideas and validation of our intent to move forward on this issue.

We then met with our longtime community leaders to get a sense of why our diversity capabilities were important to them. Hearing from them firsthand about how much value they placed on our police service not only appearing diverse but also being diverse—two different things—clarified and endorsed, or adjusted, some of our thinking. Then, we asked our own members to participate in focus groups and workshops to discuss why diversity was important to them.

During these various research steps, we discovered that reflecting the community and its diversity wasn't the issue. It wouldn't add any value to the community or to our organization to hire people simply because they looked a certain way. It wasn't how we looked that would work in developing better relationships with our community. It was rather how well connected we could be to the community that mattered. We also discovered that by recruiting from our diverse communities, with the goal of achieving connectivity within the community, the reflection would come as a matter of course.

Ultimately, we also discovered that more diversity didn't mean we had to know all the languages and represent all the cultures within the city. But we definitely had to have the capabilities available to us to connect with all of them, if required. So we developed partnerships with organizations that provided those services to us.

The message was loud and clear from everyone involved that our ability to work with the community was directly linked to our ability to communicate and connect with them beyond the business side of the relationship. This could only be done by being connected to the community in many ways, not only in acknowledging that there were different groups or communities within the city but also by living with diversity as equal partners in the community's growth.

By including as many people as possible in the discovery process, we established their buy-in and were able to announce our need for a workplace diversity plan.

Lesson 2

The Thing about Research

Everyone who is about to embark on an organizational change process should do some research first. We did extensive research but there were issues with it that caused us some concern. We discovered that there were many organizations around the world that claimed to do important work in diversity and inclusivity but that really only scratched the surface. Others made statements of claim but had no substance to prove their value-added. For others, it was not clear if they even truly had done what they claimed.

Ultimately, excellent research should capture real-life examples that reflect the desires of clients and employees. It should eliminate the possibility of wasting our time reinventing a process or approach that has already been tried—successfully or not—by someone else.

When we started our research, it was amazing what we heard from the community and our employees. The research showed how connected the two groups were to each other about their concerns. This was a consolation to me as it showed that we were not so disconnected from each other after all.

Types of Research

There are several types of research that can be done: best practices, internal and external. We used all of them to find out how diversity management had been implemented elsewhere.

Best Practices

When it comes to best practices research, the key is to determine if these practices really are best and not just statements of claim. There were instances where I found excellent statements that claimed certain actions or beliefs in diversity management in organizations or companies. But there was very little proof to support that they had actually done anything to reflect the statement. When asking them whom I could talk to about how they achieved their goal and how the programs were working for them, they either didn't call back or couldn't provide the name of a person who was responsible for the implementation and management of the program.

Then there were those organizations or companies that apparently had excellent programs but only because they had been forced by the courts to implement them because of blatant discrimination or biases, which had been proven in court.

There were some organizations that did a good job at creating and managing change at first but then slid back to where they had started. These examples showed us what could happen if the commitment to diversity change is not entrenched within the framework of how business is done but is merely superficial. There could be reasons for the failure: 1) a change in management or in the market or 2) diversity management was assigned to a section that did not have the authority to keep it on the priority list in the business plan.

This is not to say that best practices research revealed nothing of practical use. The fact that the research revealed various organizations and their actions, or non-actions, reinforced to us that we had to commit to entrenching this project and assigning people to be responsible for the actions we decided to take. There are many organizations that do a good job at what they claim. But it is necessary to sort out the claims of excellence from the real deal.

Internal Research

The next step we took involved a variety of internal research processes.

Existing practices, policies and procedures: We reviewed all our policies and procedures to ensure they were inclusive, respectful and discrimination-free. We reviewed all our training content as well. It was through this review we realized that there were issues with how we handled public complaints, managed our harassment and discrimination-free policies, our recruiting process and our new recruit coaching program. Each of these areas was then assigned a sub-project of its own to resolve the issues around each of them.

Workshops with internal groups: First, I want to start by sharing a mistake we made. To help us understand what diversity meant to all our members, we held some internal focus groups to discuss various issues. We asked questions such as: What does diversity and inclusivity mean to you? What are the facts surrounding diversity and inclusivity? What are the fallacies? What's in it for me?

These questions were discussed to get the issues about diversity out in the open and to deal with them before we started to look at implementing a plan.

For some reason, as manager of the project, I did not include white males as part of these focus groups, which was very quickly pointed out to me by the police association that represented the majority of employees. If I was going to make the claim that workplace diversity was about equality and inclusivity, then I couldn't ignore the thoughts and concerns of any group within the organization. Inclusivity means everyone not just some! In this case, I was ignoring the thoughts, concerns and values that white males could offer to the project.

This type of error can involve any group with regard to gender, age, economic status, religion and so on. Whatever the diversity component, I should have ensured considering everyone's point of view. In the end, I wandered over to the association's office, met with the president, offered my apologies and a plan to correct the mistake on my part. They then supported my efforts to gather information from this group as well.

We held internal focus groups with a variety of members who reflected both the organizational demographics and the hierarchy. This was a positive experience and the information that was shared was phenomenal and very revealing to those in charge of the project. Just some words of caution that all groups be included in these discussions.

Telephone interviews: Some employees told us that they wanted to share their thoughts but were uncomfortable attending a focus group or couldn't attend for other reasons. We conducted telephone interviews with them.

External Research

There were several types of external research available to us.

Using the local university or college: Hearing that we were involved in an organizationwide change project, a well-respected local Carleton University professor, Dr. Linda Duxbury, offered her doctoral students to us as researchers. We were concerned about addressing the question, How well prepared would our leaders be in managing the change needed to make the organization successful at diversity and inclusivity?

The students provided us with six major documents on managing change, one of which was selected by the executive as required reading for all executive members. It was to be the basis on which management moved the organization forward as a result of the project's recommendations.

Community focus groups: Knowing that whatever we did would affect the public in general, and because workplace diversity and inclusivity meant involving everyone, we decided to hear what the public had to say about the issues before we started to make changes.

In partnership with our already existing community and police action committee, referred to as COMPAC, we selected several locations throughout the city, set dates and times, contacted our community partners and put up posters on local bulletin boards to announce facilitated workshops on our efforts to create a more diverse workplace. All of these were well attended and the enthusiasm was phenomenal.

The Findings

On completion of our research, we ended up with ninety-nine recommendations for consideration, many of which were duplicative. The volunteers in COMPAC, along with members of my project team, culled all of them to reach seventeen core recommendations. Implementing these would help propel us into the future with a healthy approach to diversity and connect us to the community as we had never been before. Four of them were police-organization specific and the other thirteen were general enough in nature to fit into any organization's diversity perspective. They were:

1. Create a permanent organizational Diversity Advisory Council (DAC), whose role will be to ensure that diversity is an integral part of every aspect of management policies and practices.

2. Develop a comprehensive internal and external communications strategy to support the goals for diversification.

3. Establish measurable diversity goals and tracking mechanisms.

4. Perform a comprehensive review of the recruitment processes, with the objective to remove barriers to diversity hiring, which is consistent and bias-free.

5. Establish a mechanism to ensure that all recruitment interviewers understand and demonstrate competencies in valuing diversity, flexibility, leadership and service orientation.

6. Develop a plan to review all policies and procedures to ensure that they are fully inclusive and respect diversity.

7. Develop a formal employee orientation program for all new employees.

8. Develop an employee mentoring program that recognizes the needs of a diverse workplace.

9. Review dependent-care initiatives that reflect the needs of the employees.

10. Establish processes and a framework to support supervisory accountability to address inappropriate employee behaviour with respect to workplace harassment and discrimination.

11. Integrate diversity content into all training.

12. Bolster existing or, where warranted, establish formal and informal mediation mechanisms for public complaints.

13. Establish a supervisor selection process that includes competencies in valuing diversity, flexibility, leadership, communication and service orientation.

By conducting different types of research, we were able to include as many groups as possible in discussing issues around diversity and come up with recommendations.

Lesson 3

Establish the Environment for Workplace Diversity

Those of us working on the project realized that, before we went about attracting people to our organization, we had to make sure the existing environment was welcoming and supportive of our current diversified and talented workforce. Ultimately, we knew that, if we weren't already taking care of our own people, people would visit but nobody would want to stay.

I was reminded of the story of the person who passes away and faces two choices—to go to heaven or to Hades. When presented with heaven, he finds an environment that is peaceful, quaint and delightful. He then visits Hades and finds that everyone there is partying, playing sports and enjoying life to its fullest. The next day, he decides that, if given the choice, he will go to Hades. Heaven closes its gates to him and he goes to Hades where, as the gates open, he is faced with pain and suffering, and the worst living conditions imaginable. Where, he asks his guide, are all the exciting and fun things he saw in Hades yesterday. To which the guide replies, "Oh, yes, well yesterday we were recruiting; today you work for us."

When I hear recruiters state that the only plan they have to add more diversity to the workplace is to simply recruit more diverse-looking candidates, I worry about the organization and the new employees from several perspectives.

- It should not be the responsibility of these new vulnerable employees to reach out to current employees to teach them to accept and celebrate their differences.

- Changes that are required to make demographic diversity work do not happen through osmosis. We may add diversity but that doesn't mean the existing group becomes diverse. The current group may simply force newcomers to become the same as what is already there.

- When we recruit to attract unique talent and give the impression that ours is a welcoming and respectful organization to work for, it had better be; otherwise, as a business owner, we may be unwittingly misleading the candidate into a false sense of well-being and, in effect, creating a psychological breach of contract that may lead to more serious legal repercussions and very expensive costs.

- Policies and procedures that address how discrimination and harassment-free environments are managed and supported are the organization's responsibility to develop. They are not for new hires to look for and demand once they are employed.

It was a huge task to identify how our organization welcomed and supported diversity in its workplace but was well worth the effort. We reviewed:

- how we went about attracting people to policing;

- our hiring process;

- our mentorship program (We called it the Coach Officer Program, as our recruits spent up to twelve months or more with experienced officers to gain comfort in the practical application of all the theory they had learned at the police college.);

- our workplace harassment and discrimination policy to make it more supportive rather than disciplinary and to encourage our supervisors to work to improve situations rather that feel threatened if they failed to do something (It was our belief that when a policy is based on discipline and threats, staff will hide the problem. But when it is built on support and training, then they will work toward improving the environment.);

- our support for continuing education;

- how we accommodated employees with family care issues;

- our communications strategy; and

- our public and internal complaint process.

We were trying to make diversity and inclusivity a normal part of the way we did business and to reach a point where this was the norm among our staff. We wanted to ensure that each individual's unique talent was recognized and that everyone would be encouraged to listen to and consider new and innovative ways of thinking in order to move the organization forward to be more competitive and to serve its clients better. We wanted every person in the organization to be involved in the transition for change for the sake of growth and not simply for the sake of change.

By the time we were ready to announce new hiring initiatives to attract more diverse employees, current employees should already be working in an environment where people look forward to these new hires and are already aware of and anxious for the value-added these individuals will bring to the team and to the organization overall.

Once the issues around diversity in the current work environment are addressed, if recruiting is the next right step, then happy recruiting!

Lesson 4

Review the Recruiting Process

There are two major stages to the recruiting process. The first stage is to attract candidates and the second one is the hiring process itself.

The First Stage

We discovered that there was talent in the community. But this talent did not see how it could fit into our organization. So it was up to our organization to show these talented, unique and diverse people why our organization was worth working for and how they were a fit with us. It was now a matter of attracting them differently than we were used to by using traditional means, so we initiated several things.

We started a Champion Program (*see* illustration 1) that was intended to ensure we reached out to everyone. We started by offering information sessions that addressed most people's questions and concerns. This led to one-on-one coaching and support, if any individual required further clarification about the recruiting process.

It was our understanding, as a result of meeting with community leaders during our initial research phase, that, unless we put the effort into reaching out to the various communities, we were not going to connect with some good potential candidates. They simply were not attracted to policing initially. The days of shopping mall recruitment booths, newspaper advertisements and the twice-a-year university or college job fairs just didn't meet our needs anymore.

Illustration 1: Recruitment Champion

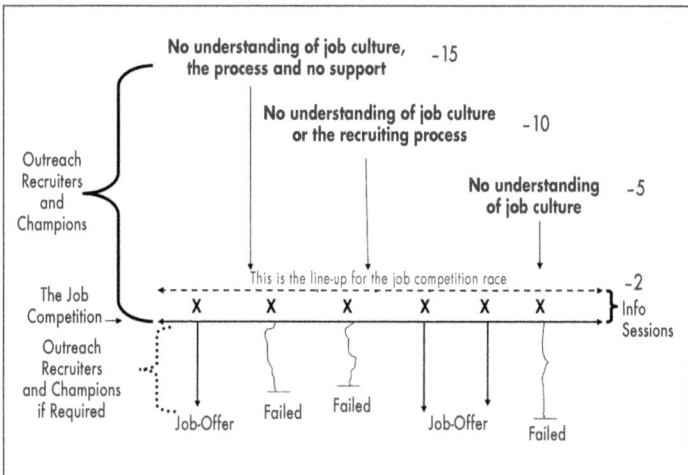

The days of simply processing applications from the filing cabinet were now long gone.

It wasn't our intent to convince people to become police officers. There has to be a strong desire to join the police service. But it was our belief that the policing spirit existed in many of our new community members; we simply needed to learn how to reach out to it, nurture it and, at the same time, bring about organizational change that would support it.

There were four stages that we focused on when meeting members from minority communities:

1. the applicant's clear understanding of the job and its expectations,

2. an understanding of the competitive process into which they will enter,

3. the reality of the job and

4. support through the process and on the job.

To understand how much effort we would have to put into getting a candidate into the hiring stages, I developed terminology that worked for me. I called it the Zero, Minus Five, Minus Ten and Minus Fifteen stages. This is not language that was used universally or even in my office. It simply helped me to understand the level of effort I would have to assign to a candidate.

If I saw that an applicant didn't understand the competitive process, the reality of the job or the consequences of becoming a police officer in their community, I saw them at the Minus Fifteen stage. These applicants needed a lot of effort on our part to make sure they understood what they were getting into and what would be required of them every step along the hiring process and on the job itself.

If they didn't understand the competitive process or the reality of the job, but understood the consequences of becoming a police officer in their community, I saw them at the Minus Ten stage. They needed a targeted effort on our part to make sure they understood what they were getting into, compared to what they thought they were getting into.

If the applicants didn't understand the competitive process but understood the reality of the job and the consequences of becoming a police officer in their community, I saw them at the Minus Five stage. They only needed support in working their way through the recruitment process and help in clarifying what to expect next.

If they had a strong understanding of the job, its expectations, the competitive process and the reality of the job, and had someone to go to for clarification or explanations, I saw them at the Zero stage. They needed no effort on our part to see them through the process. Most applicants from the pool, who had submitted their application on their own and attended any of our public information sessions, were at the Zero stage.

The objective of the Champion Program was to ensure that all the candidates who applied were at the Zero stage. In other words, everyone, who was trying to be hired for a position against thirty other people also applying for the same position, had to feel confident that they are as informed, prepared and qualified as they could be for what they had to do or know to win that position.

The other step we took was to increase our visibility at community events and functions in order to connect with the youth in the communities.

All of these efforts, beyond our traditional ones, gained us much in the way of connectivity with potentially new and diverse employees.

The Second Stage

In the late 1990s, the Ontario Police College, in cooperation with the Ontario Association of Chiefs of Police, determined that the testing procedures for police applicants had to be changed to meet bona fide occupational requirements. The college even took its newly developed tests to the courts to ensure that they were bias-free and job-related. Not everyone can go to such lengths; however, at the very least, all recruiting processes should be bona fide and job-related.

I was once told by a small business manager that he had some concerns about age when it came to hiring employees for his warehouse; there was a lot of heavy lifting involved. He determined that, if an applicant was over a certain age, he wouldn't even consider them for a position. But he had no test in place to determine how capable an individual might be at lifting weight and moving heavy items around. As a result, many people in their fifties, who were in excellent physical shape and who would have passed a physical test without any difficulty, were not even considered for work in the warehouse by this manager.

Although it was not intended, he was discriminating against age and ignoring a lot of potential talent and wisdom that age can bring. Today, with so many highly talented and skilled people retiring early, and looking for opportunities to do simpler jobs to keep themselves busy or to supplement their pensions, he had no idea of the phenomenal talent he was throwing away by making such an arbitrary decision in his recruiting process.

To ensure that we were being fair and open-minded, we convened a series of panel sessions that brought together a diverse group of community leaders and some of our employees to review our hiring processes. They found no problems with the testing processes that had been established by the Ontario Association of Chiefs of Police and our adherence to the steps. We were then able to launch a communications plan to address specific issues of misunderstanding about our testing process from some community members.

Lesson 5

When we first started our journey toward becoming a more diverse organization, I found some of the terminology commonly used such as diversity, inclusivity, equity and equality, both confusing and conflicting. It surprised me how these words meant different things to different people within the same organization. In our case, there were five key words and related concepts that needed to be clear to everyone in order to move forward.

Diversity

Diversity can mean different things to different people. It was quite an eye-opener for me to realize that I would be having a conversation with someone at work about diversity only to discover we weren't even starting in our conversation with the same understanding of its meaning. I would be talking about discovering the hidden talent needed to help us connect to the community. The other person would be talking in terms of how we looked to the community to connect, regardless of the hidden talent. I also discovered that, for some people, talking about diversity simply meant talking about issues with someone from a designated group. It did not include the bigger picture of diversity being all-inclusive.

The view of diversity that offers the greatest opportunity for innovative and creative ways of doing business includes far more than the four categories of visible minorities, women, persons with disabilities and Aboriginal people, in other words, far more than what is seen at a glance. Diversity includes recognizing not only the primary dimensions but also the secondary dimensions of people as well.

Primary and Secondary Dimensions

When considering workplace diversity and achieving connectivity to our clients, we need to take into account both the primary dimensions of diversity, which are those things that we see in people, and the secondary dimensions, which are those things that we don't see. It is in the dimensions we don't see that many of the unique talents of individuals are found. In some cases we both see and don't see certain dimensions of diversity such as a person's sexual orientation, religion or socioeconomic status.

The secondary dimensions of language, socioeconomic background, religion, education, sexual orientation, family structure, experience and the many other wide-ranging facets make each of us unique. These dimensions are far more value-added than just being satisfied with recruiting those with a different skin colour. (Illustration 2 shows disabilities in both the primary and secondary dimensions as there are both visible and hidden disabilities in people.)

Illustration 2: Dimensions of Diversity

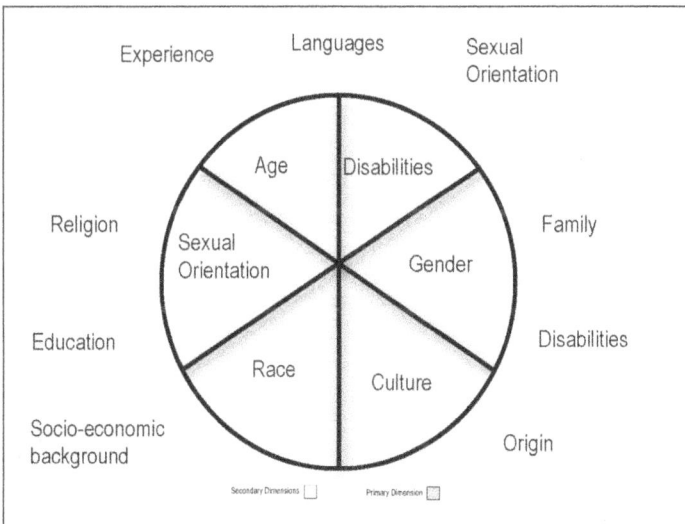

Source: ©1996. *Implementing Diversity* by Marilyn Loden. McGraw-Hill Publishing, Burr Ridge, IL. Reprinted with author's permission.

Excellence in diversity not only looks like the community but is also connected to the community.

Equality and Equity: Both Working Together!

Equality is the foundation piece to establishing a diversified workplace. We want everyone to be treated with the same end result, that is, with respect and fairness for everyone. Because not everyone is the same, this means that we have to come up with different ways of treating some people (equity) to get the end result of equal treatment for everyone (equality), including for those who are different.

There are many examples of how we are different from each other. Addressing how we deal with these differences is where we sometimes confuse equality with equity. Some will say that, because we are treating someone differently, they are getting preferential treatment over others. In fact, the difference in how we treat them (equity) is simply taking steps to treat them as fairly and as equally as others who don`t need this different approach (equality).

Everyone wants, and is entitled, to be treated with respect and fairness. How we deal with a person, so they feel respected and fairly treated, may be different from one group to another and even from one individual to another. Ultimately, even though all our approaches may be different (equity), we should be trying to achieve the same end result (equality)—that the person feels respected and fairly treated regardless of what they believe in. How we manage and communicate equity, however, can be difficult if people don't understand how these two concepts work hand in hand.

As an example, when we (the police service) were recruiting, we often held open-house information sessions at our local college. Many members of our ethnic communities would not attend these sessions because they didn't understand police work and would have to ask too many questions at the session about this career choice. They thought they would be viewed as disruptive and naïve by the majority of those who attended; they wouldn`t come even though they were interested. So we held information sessions with potentially highly skilled and talented ethnic community members in environments in which they were comfortable and at locations they offered in which to meet their potential candidates.

These information sessions could be seen as treating these ethnic communities in a special way compared to what everyone else was being offered; however, these sessions were nothing more than the equal and fair exchange of the same information with everyone but recognizing the need for a different format. Although this meant more work for managers, the benefit to our organization was an investment of time worth making.

Inclusivity

Inclusivity is about *including* everyone in the workplace and not limiting our efforts only to certain designated or targeted groups of people. For such a change to occur in an organization, plans should be made with a view to the future and not with a focus on correcting past mistakes. Thus, implementing this type of project, with the idea of changing the workplace environment by focusing on one specific minority group to the disadvantage of a majority in the workplace, will create little goodwill and probably considerable resentment. If anyone or any group feels that they are not included as part of the change process or the organization's desire to become more diverse, then inclusivity has not been achieved.

Demographic Diversity

Demography is the statistical study of human populations and subpopulations. In its most general application, it refers to measuring everything that is different about people, as well as taking into consideration changes that occur over time.

Demographic diversity is everything about a person's make-up, or an organization's infrastructure or a country's way of doing business that makes it or them absolutely unique, with time as an added component. For example, two years ago, I was a father and spouse;

today, I am a father, spouse and grandfather. Today, I am more demographically diverse than I was two years ago. I now have a grandfather's perspective.

Demographic diversity can also measure everything that is different about how businesses work in different countries, whether they are all built on the same basic principles of obtaining the best return on their investments. As an example, one year ago, an organization consisted of one head office and twenty-three branch offices throughout North America. Today, it has branch offices in Africa and South America. Today, it is more demographically capable of competing in more diverse ways than it was last year. Today, it has employees and customers who work in environments with influences and perspectives from other countries that they didn't have last year.

This same diversity applies to people. It never occurred to me how complex, unique and ever-changing we are as individuals until I saw the growth in my two sons over the last thirty years. They were born fourteen months apart and given exactly the same upbringing and experiences as a result of everything we did together as a family. I thought they would have a fairly similar approach to life. Yet they are such different and unique adults in their approach and thoughts to issues and situations that, unless you knew they were brothers, you wouldn't know they even knew each other. It's almost as if they were raised in two different families worlds apart.

As a business, knowing how the world is changing in relation to the talent we have to work with in our organization, how work is done in certain countries and how customers are reacting to our products or services at any given time is paramount to our survival and ability to thrive going forward. Ensuring the business, or organization, has a diversified workforce, where everyone is treated equally and valued for their uniqueness, will provide the best opportunities for us to meet and overcome challenges.

Lesson 6

ESTABLISH A LEVEL OF AWARENESS

ABOUT WORKPLACE DIVERSITY

Knowing what our level of awareness is about workplace diversity, what it can do for us and what it means as a business owner will help determine where the starting point is for the change process for growth. This knowledge will also help with the communications strategy and in determining whether the change is simply about nurturing the existing workplace diversity or expanding on it, or both.

When the Ottawa Police Service first became involved in the workplace diversity process for our organization, we were truly unaware of what it was we were trying to accomplish. We really thought it was a simple recruitment project.

To help explain what we mean by establishing our level of awareness about workplace diversity, I'll refer to the illustration titled "Conscious Competence Learning Matrix." (*See* illustration 3.)

Our organizational level of awareness on starting this project was in the lower left quadrant at the *Unconscious Incompetence* level. As we spoke with people in the organization trying to become more connected with our clients (i.e., the community), we started to realize that we didn't know what we needed

Illustration 3: Conscious Competence Learning Matrix

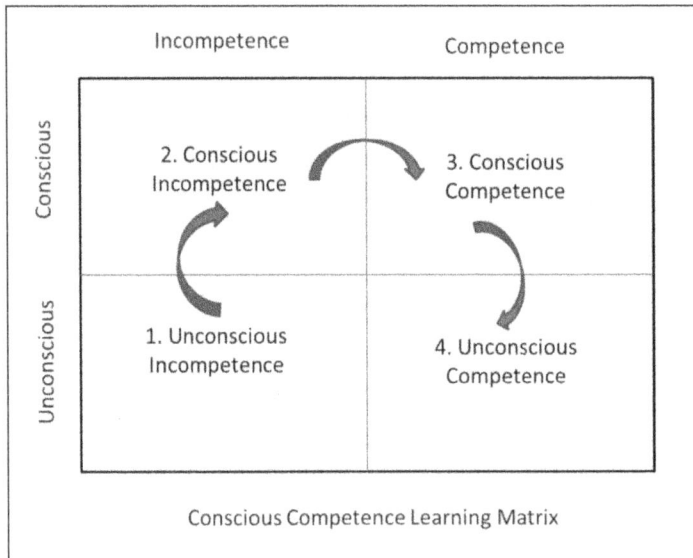

	Incompetence	Competence
Conscious	2. Conscious Incompetence	3. Conscious Competence
Unconscious	1. Unconscious Incompetence	4. Unconscious Competence

Conscious Competence Learning Matrix

Source: The four stages of competence are taken from:
http://en.wikipedia.org/wiki/Four stages of competence.

to know. At this point, we moved to the upper left quadrant to the *Conscious Incompetence* level.

As we began our research, listened to experts in the field of workplace diversity and attended workshops and conferences on diversity issues, we started to become passionate about the work we had previously panicked about. We started to learn what it was we needed to do and, at the same time, we were creating some changes in the workplace. We had now moved into the upper right quadrant of *Conscious Competence.*

We never reached a point in our organization where we did things to be inclusive without having to think about them. This would have meant an *Unconscious Competence* level of awareness (*see* the lower right quadrant in the illustration). Not having reached this level doesn't mean it can't be done, it just wasn't something our organization managed to accomplish.

We should expect to find a wide range of awareness levels among individuals and at various levels of management throughout the organization. The more the variance, the more complex the process required to address the levels of awareness.

Lesson 7

REVIEW WORKPLACE DISCRIMINATION AND HARASSMENT-FREE POLICIES

To ensure that the environment is a safe and welcoming one for current employees, as well as for new employees, we need to review the existing workplace discrimination and harassment policies. We must also ensure that everyone, especially supervisors, is given the training they need to make certain the workplace is indeed discrimination- and harassment-free.

The key here is accountability. No matter how well developed a policy is, it can't succeed if people aren't held accountable at various stages of implementing and adhering to it. We also found it difficult to manage workplace and harassment-free policies, when the actions to correct failures were punitive, so we considered a positive approach to discrimination and harassment management. We turned the existing process of punishment into one of conciliation, negotiation and facilitation when addressing conflicts. This led to end results that were agreed on, whether they were remedial or corrective measures rather than punitive.

There are dozens of organizations that offer training for supervisors and assistance in policy and procedure development in the area of managing discrimination and harassment in the workplace. If this is not something we can do on our own, we should consider contacting one of these organizations for assistance.

Lesson 8

COMMUNICATIONS IS A GREAT TOOL – USE IT!

The bottom line is that actions do speak louder than words! So communications is an important tool to help create successful workplace diversity.

Our police chief shared the following with me:

> There was this farmer's field in which lived a wild turkey. This turkey always had the dream of one day being able to fly to the top of the tree, which was located in the centre of the cleared field. Also living in this field was a large bull. The bull had been watching the efforts of the turkey. One day he spoke to the turkey, "Within my droppings are the nutrients that you need to fly to the top of the tree. You must eat my droppings."
>
> The turkey accepted the advice and started eating the bull's droppings. After a few weeks of eating this way, he suddenly found the strength to make it to the top of the

tree. He was so proud of his success that he let out a long and loud, "gobble, gobble, gobble" for all to hear.

Indeed, everyone did hear, including the farmer who, not knowing that there had been a wild turkey in the field, was now pleased to hear and see it. He immediately grabbed his shotgun and shot the turkey down from the tree to make a fine meal for him and his family.

The chief stopped for a moment to let me think about the story. He then went on to state that the moral of this story is, although bullshit may get us to where we want to be, it will not sustain us there for very long.

It was advice I never forgot whenever we communicated any information about the goals and objectives we were trying to accomplish in addressing workplace diversity. It is vital to speak the truth at all times. Depending on how complex the organization is, communications can be a critical component. The following tips are offered on how to use communications to our advantage.

Tip #1: Be Aware of the 15 – 70 –15 Rule

Depending on the size of the organization, the 15-70-15 rule may or may not be a factor to consider (*See* illustration 4). But for those who need it, what this rule means is that we will generally find that there are fifteen percent of the people we work with who will

Illustration 4: The 15 – 70 –15 Rule

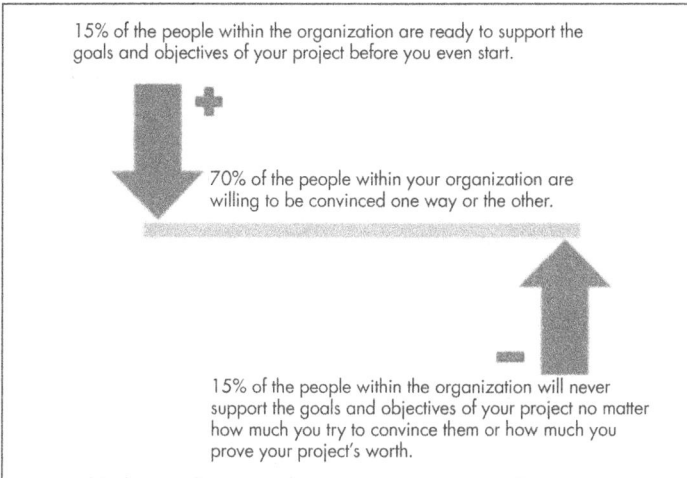

15% of the people within the organization are ready to support the goals and objectives of your project before you even start.

70% of the people within your organization are willing to be convinced one way or the other.

15% of the people within the organization will never support the goals and objectives of your project no matter how much you try to convince them or how much you prove your project's worth.

support—almost unequivocally—the objectives and benefits of workplace diversity. This group is already convinced that what we are about to start is something that should have been done already. At the other end, we will find fifteen percent in the organization who will never accept workplace diversity as having any merit or value.

In between, we have seventy percent of the workforce just waiting to be convinced or informed about the value of diversity to the workplace. We should take advantage of the opportunity to talk to this group as soon as possible; they are waiting to hear from us. If we don't follow up with them, they may become part of the fifteen percent who are negative about change. It is always easier to be dismissive about a project requiring change than it is to get involved and work with it. If we wait too long, then the damage will have been done and it will be much harder to change people's attitudes.

Tip #2: Don't Mislead People

Integrity is paramount when it comes to telling the truth about what we are trying to accomplish. Some senior managers believe that only good news should be conveyed to employees. However, I discovered in our workplace diversity efforts that we received the most support from the community and staff when we revealed our weaknesses and mistakes, and our desire to address them now that they were acknowledged.

Tip #3: Make Announcements a Reason to Celebrate

We need to announce every success we have as well, no matter how small it may seem. I met with the executive of another major police service to talk about why we, in Ottawa, were perceived as being so successful with our workplace diversity efforts, when their organization wasn't, even though they had many more successful accomplishments than we did in the area of diversity management.

What was revealed in discussions was that very few in

their organization or in their community knew about their work in the area of diversity, since they didn't incorporate a communications strategy in their plan, which celebrated their successes. Therefore, it appeared both in their organization and in their community that they had done very little, or nothing at all, to create the changes they needed. It's important to brag about ourselves!

Tip #4: Use Your Own People to Support Your Communications Efforts

One of the best things we did was to communicate comments from our staff that showed their support for the work we were doing. Nothing reinforces the efforts of an organizational change project as strongly as support at the grassroots level.

Tip #5: Answer Every Challenge Positively

As in every organization, our water-cooler gossip network was healthy. Every now and then, someone would start a negative rumour about the work we were trying to accomplish. Many times, however, rumours start as a result of strongly held beliefs, which may be based on perception only. Yet, for many, perception is reality, so regardless of how offensive the rumour may be, there is usually a reason for it, which many believe validates their concerns.

If someone takes time to challenge our work, it is probably because they feel strongly enough about it to express their own thoughts and beliefs. This is a compliment because our work means something to them.

We need to take the time to respond to any rumours that are circulating in relation to the work being done. We should thank staff for expressing their concerns and provide the facts about what we are doing. This helps to negate their concerns. We shouldn't respond by giving a non-answer. People are fed up with this type of non-response and won't accept this kind of manipulation.

On the other hand, if we don't respond at all, we take a chance on losing some of the seventy percent of the organization who are neutral to the fifteen percent who are negative.

Tip #6: Share the Results with Others

We need to share any results we learn with staff. They will applaud these efforts to connect with them.

When we did our internal workforce census, for example, we discovered things about our organization that we didn't know. Best of all, we found out that we had more diversity in our organization than we thought. As a result of sharing this information with our community of clients, they acknowledged that we had a good starting point on which to build and they encouraged us to do more.

Very quickly, after the organization showed some signs that things were changing, community groups were not only speaking more highly of us than ever before but also wanted to help by getting involved in our recruiting efforts.

Lesson 9

THE BUSINESS CASE

When an organization is about to fundamentally change how it operates, there can be anxiety, stress, uneasiness and worry within the existing workplace. There certainly was in our organization. It takes a sustained commitment of time and effort by the entire business or organization to address these reactions. This is why it is important to develop a business case for creating a diverse workplace.

Essentially, a business case is a strategic plan that takes advantage of an opportunity to create change. In our organization, a number of retirements were occurring at a time when there was more diversity within the community than we had ever seen in previous years. Therefore, this offered us an opportunity to reach out to the community to replace the large numbers of people who were retiring. At the same time that we were taking advantage of an opportunity, we were also meeting a need—to increase our effectiveness as a service to the community by being more diverse and by giving ourselves the competitive advantage when it came to providing that service.

There is a basic flow to how a business case rolls out. The first phase is to establish the case for change that clearly defines the need for the investment. The second phase consists of acquiring a wide range of change options to achieve the goals defined in the first phase. Then, it is a matter of analyzing these options to see which can be achieved and which are the best options to meet the established goals. Once this is done, then it's a matter of making recommendations that can be initiated to achieve the goals. Finally, the third phase is to manage and evaluate the changes.

There are seven keys to success in rolling out a business case. They are:

1. Determine who should be the project's champion (*see* Lesson 11).

2. Determine who should manage the project (*see* Lesson 10).

3. Understand who is responsible for the project's overall success (*see* Lesson 3). Ultimately, every

manager in each division, sector or department is responsible, not just human resources.

4. Involve everyone in the project for change.

5. Ensure that everyone has an opportunity to be engaged throughout the project.

6. Set up a process for obtaining constant feedback as the project progresses.

7. Develop a project that is flexible enough to make changes, if necessary, but that is not so flexible it allows the project's scope to creep beyond its mandate.

Each and every one of these keys to success is addressed in this book.

Lesson 10

PICK THE RIGHT MANAGER FOR THE PROCESS

Knowing who should manage the process of creating workplace diversity and why that person is the right one is crucial to its success. For smaller companies or businesses, there may be no choice as to who will manage the process. It will be either the owner or the manager. But regardless of who manages, there are some things that this person needs to know about the skills required to manage the workplace diversity process.

Based on my experiences, successful management of workplace diversity initiatives has very little to do with a person's positional power in the organization and much more to do with personal power. It definitely has everything to do with an individual's personal stamina and ability to accomplish tasks in a passionately charged environment.

Positional and Personal Power

Generally, those who rely solely on positional power to get things done have poor people skills. They count on their position within the organization to ensure things get done the way they want them to be done. Often, they are not easy to like or to get along with but they do get the job done. The downside is that, when these managers are not on-site to enforce their decisions, people tend to ignore what has been accomplished thus far and do what they thought they should have done initially.

Managers who work only with personal power have good people skills. They inspire people to behave or react in certain ways simply because they are liked and their opinions are respected. However, the downside is that, when tough decisions have to be made, if they can't convince people to respond voluntarily, then, sometimes, they can't get people to respond at all and their leadership status falls apart.

The most desirable person to be in charge of a project, where change is required and emotions may be involved, is one who has demonstrated both strong personal power and good positional power to a varying degree.

I am often asked how I managed to work with the association (for police officers) in undertaking this project to create change in the police service. For me, it was a matter of trust and respect on the part of the association members. I had worked the streets with my peers for twenty years and had not only gained their respect but I had also acquired respect for them. And I was still a member of the association. As a staff sergeant, I held the highest rank in the association membership, so I was part of their structure and aware of their concerns because they were mine as well.

To ensure their participation, I offered the police association (union) a seat on the project's steering committee. At each stage, they had an opportunity to express their concerns to me directly at committee meetings. I made a commitment, backed up by the executive, that no phase of the project would go forward unless we reached consensus at the steering committee meeting, which included association members.

Managing by Consensus

A key skill for a successful manager in implementing change in the workplace is being able to manage through consensus. Consensus is both a process and an outcome. It is a process in which everyone has his or her say. Differing views are fully addressed and resolved by the team. A satisfactory level of agreement emerges, which is acceptable to everyone. Consensus does not necessarily mean one-hundred-percent agreement from all parties. A decision arrived at by consensus is one that the team can live with and agrees to support. Although the process of reaching consensus among many is lengthier than decisions taken by individuals, the level of commitment to a decision and its implementation is stronger.

Where consensus is the chosen method for reaching a decision, participants must keep working to understand each other's perspectives until they develop a shared framework of understanding. They provide input from their various points of view and the likelihood of introducing new, creative solutions is positive. Consensus is by far the most time-consuming approach to decision-making and takes the most effort. Properly managed, consensus agreements have the best chance of producing sustainable results when the stakes are high. Participants reach a level of agreement they can support and are more committed to the outcome because they were actively involved in developing the solution.

In situations where the stakes are low, consensus has been rated as equivalent to other decision-making processes in terms of its quality. Participants are encouraged to go along with proposals that they can tolerate if decisions are made without consensus, instead of finding the best innovative solution. This would require considerable time and effort. The use of consensus for low-stakes decisions can prevent a group from making decisions that would not be tolerated by a small minority.

Some drawbacks to the consensus process are:

1. This is a time-consuming process.

2. There is a general tendency for groups to push for fast decisions.

3. Pressure from some participants may force others to live with decisions that they don't truly support.

4. The committee ends up with diluted compromises instead of high-quality decisions.

As a diligent manager, I watched for these signs and encouraged the active participation of all parties.

In summary, consensus is a process for finding a proposal acceptable enough that all committee members can support it and where no member opposes it outright. Consensus is not a unanimous vote or a majority vote, and not everyone involved is totally satisfied. Finally, consensus requires time; the active participation of all committee members; skills in communication, that is, listening, conflict resolution, discussion facilitation; and creative thinking and open-mindedness.

In managing the consensus process and validating the decisions reached, I would then summarize the group's position on an issue, state the decision that seemed to have been made and check whether the team agreed with the summary. All consensus decisions were recorded in meeting minutes.

Management Competencies and Personality Traits

The next step is to identify what competencies and personality traits are required in the manager who is selected to implement workplace changes.

Competencies

The competencies required for a project manager to lead organizational change are listed in detail in the following table.

Table 1: Competencies Required to Manage Workplace Diversity

COMPETENCY	SKILLS
Communication	• Scans the environment for key information and messages in the development of communication strategies for the project. • Communicates strategically to achieve specific objectives (optimal messaging and timing). • Uses varied communication methods and opportunities to promote dialogue and develop shared understanding and consensus. • Displays confidence and self-assurance when communicating project strategies.
Teamwork	• Actively builds cooperation among multiple teams within the project. • Promotes teamwork between their own project teams and other teams throughout the organization. • Promotes sharing of expertise among project teams.

COMPETENCY	SKILLS
Adaptability	• Adjusts the strategic directions of the project to address a diverse range of situations. • Effectively shifts priorities and associated project strategies to respond quickly to emerging opportunities and risks.
Project Orientation	• Looks for long-term benefits and adjusts approach accordingly, even at a cost, for the sake of the project's success. • Identifies emerging organizational needs and incorporates them into the project. • Develops and maintains an in-depth understanding of the project's needs and objectives. • When appropriate, includes others from outside the project in the decision-making process.
Networking and Relationship Building	• Creates a formal network to influence the success of the project. • Brokers relationships within the organization to achieve the project's strategic priorities. • Regularly evaluates existing contacts to renew networks, identifying new relationships to be developed in order to ensure the project's strategic objectives can be attained. • Uses networks to identify strategic opportunities and to resolve complex problems. • Creates a positive image and reputation for the organization through relationships and networks.
Problem Solving	• Anticipates and prepares for long-term opportunities or problems. • Develops comprehensive solutions to complex problems. • Thinks beyond the project and into the future, balancing multiple perspectives when setting directions or reaching conclusions.

COMPETENCY	SKILLS
Leadership	• Inspires and mentors others through their own positive attitude and energy at work. • Seeks leadership opportunities and accepts related responsibilities. • Recognizes their limitations and seeks improvement. • Demonstrates accountability for their own actions and decisions. • Demonstrates self-assurance and confidence. • Builds trust by being honest, reliable and consistent. • Accepts criticisms/critiques of ideas and decisions, and considers recommendations. • Admits their own mistakes and encourages others to learn from the experience. • Fulfills commitments, even under difficult or challenging circumstances. • Addresses behaviours that contravene the project's core values and mission. • Behaves with integrity, making principled and ethical decisions, even if they are sensitive or controversial. • Encourages others to remain focused and productive during challenging and demanding situations.
Planning and Organizing	• Oversees development and manages overall strategy, plans, resources, and systems to implement programs and policy related to the project. • Works within the plans that affect the strategic direction of the project. • Analyzes emerging opportunities and threats, and forecasts the major implications for the project. • Reallocates resources to reflect strategic risks and the priorities of the project. • Uses formal risk management processes and tools to continuously manage risk.

COMPETENCY	SKILLS
Resource and Fiscal Management	• Sets priorities around goals and objectives based on budgetary allocations and constraints. • Establishes and aligns authority, responsibility and accountability with the project's objectives. • Ensures that there is an adequate project control system over expenditures. • Prioritizes and allocates resources appropriately to meet the overall needs of the project.
Organizational Awareness	• Understands the politics, issues and external influences of organization. • Achieves solutions acceptable to varied parties based on their understanding of issues, climates and cultures in their own and other organizations. • Anticipates issues, challenges and outcomes, and effectively operates to best position the project.
Environmental Awareness	• Demonstrates a broad understanding of the social and economic context within which the project operates. • Understands and anticipates the potential trends of the political environment and the impact these might have on the project. • Operates successfully in a variety of social, political and cultural environments.
Strategic Thinking (cont'd on page 88)	• Links current programs to the longer-term perspectives of the project. • Considers the "big picture" when implementing new programs and actively researches current developments and trends. • Understands and integrates into their own thinking how factors such as technological breakthroughs, government policy, demographics, lifestyle, etc., are likely to affect the future direction of the project.

COMPETENCY	SKILLS
Strategic Thinking (cont'd from page 87)	• Integrates intelligence into a short- to medium-term plan, and articulates and executes the strategies. • Identifies what the needs will be in the short-term future and how the organization's priorities will have to change to address these emerging needs. • Identifies and seizes opportunities to address emerging cultural, social, political or organizational priorities. • Identifies, analyzes and interprets complex emerging national and international issues, and provides direction on how the organization will address these issues over the long run. • Fosters proactive thinking across the organization, and with partner agencies and governments, to address anticipated issues. • Recognizes opportunities and risks associated with different long-term organizational and interorganizational approaches to emerging issues. • Considers the common good of the organization in all decision-making, balancing the needs of the organization with the needs of their respective areas of responsibility.

These competencies are key in enabling the project manager to work with all employees in the organization to implement workplace change. Certainly, no one individual will have all of them but those listed in the table provide a list of the competencies that should be looked for in anyone who is selected to lead a project for organizational change. The larger the number of competencies demonstrated, the better the potential for a successful project manager.

Personality Traits—The DISC Model of Human Behaviour

Healthy and positive personal and work relationships develop from having an accurate, healthy and positive view of ourselves and others. There are all types of exercises to help determine if our personality compliments our positional or personal power. These exercises will also identify how personality traits impact people's behaviour in an organization. When managing a project such as workplace diversity, it is important for a manager to understand how people behave and how they are motivated.

In 1928, Dr. William Marston wrote *The Emotions of Normal People* after earning his doctorate from Harvard University. Marston theorized that people are motivated by four intrinsic drives that direct behavioural patterns. He created the Four Temperament Model of Human Behaviour, also known as the DISC Model of Human Behaviour. He used four descriptive characteristics, represented by the four letters D, I, S and C, to describe a person's behavioural tendencies. Since then, the DISC model has been used and applied in many ways to empower and equip people to apply the information for more effective communication, interaction, decision-making and understanding the priorities and the strengths of both themselves and others. (*See* illustration 5.)

The DISC Model of Human Behaviour is based on two foundational observations about how people normally behave:

Observation #1: Some people are more outgoing, while others are more reserved.

Observation #2: Some people are more task-oriented, while others are more people-oriented.

From both observations, the DISC model emphasizes that these behavioural tendencies are neither right nor wrong. They are just different. From these behavioural traits, we can further determine each of the four main personality styles and where people fall in the circle. This is a simple key to understanding how people behave and how they are motivated both personally and professionally.

Illustration 5: The DISC Model of Human Behaviour

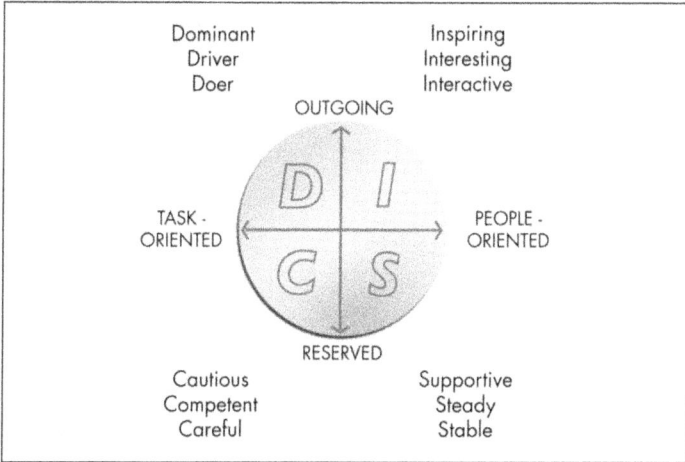

The four letters D, I, S, and C describe distinct personality traits and dominant characteristics of individuals as follows:

The Dominant D type is an outgoing, task-oriented individual who will be focused on getting things done, accomplishing tasks, getting to the bottom line as quickly as possible and making things happen. (The key insight in developing a relationship with this type of person is respect and results.)

The Inspiring I type is an outgoing, people-oriented individual who loves to interact, socialize and have fun. This person is focused on what others may think of him or her. (The key insight in developing a relationship with this type of person is admiration and recognition.)

The Supportive S type is a reserved, people-oriented individual who will enjoy relationships, helping or supporting other people and working together as a team. (The key insight in developing a relationship with this person is friendliness and sincere appreciation.)

The Cautious C type is a reserved, task-oriented individual who will seek value, consistency and quality information. This person focuses on being correct and accurate. (The key insight in developing a relationship with this individual is trust and integrity.)

To summarize the DISC Model of Human Behaviour (in order clockwise):

- D stands for the dominant type who is outgoing and task-oriented.

- I stands for the inspiring type who is outgoing and people-oriented.

- S stands for the supportive type who is reserved and people-oriented.

- C stands for the cautious type who is reserved and task-oriented.

We may often be surprised to learn which personality traits we possess. It doesn't matter if we have done any type of personality traits testing when we were in university or college; our years of experience may have shifted our skills and the environment may have shifted the weight of our personality traits. So revisiting personality traits assessment every now and then is a good idea.

According to Dr. Robert A. Rohm, president of Personality Insights in Atlanta, Georgia, and an accredited human behaviour specialist, each person's perspective is built into who they are. Some people call it personality. Some refer to it as temperament. The starting point to understanding people is to realize and accept the fact that everyone is not like us, even though we may all be trying to accomplish the same thing.

Implementing successful workplace diversity, and getting the competitive edge as a result, is all about our ability to connect with a wider range of clients. Understanding each person's personality traits and how they interact with others is a good start.

What I Discovered about Myself
Going through the testing process to identify my personality traits, prior to getting involved in managing the workplace diversity project, would have made a major difference to me and to all those involved in working with me. I would have known

my strengths and my challenges, and how they impacted others.

I would also have had other members of the police service do the exercise to learn their personality traits, using the DISC Model of Human Behaviour, so that they too would know what their strengths and challenges were.

When I did go through the evaluation process, using this model, my personality type came out as a CD/S blend, with C and D being my dominant traits and S my not so dominant trait. More research into these personality traits revealed that I had certain basic characteristics in me that were either a benefit or challenge to my leadership and to my relationship with others both in the work and the social environment. For example, both of my predominant traits indicated that I liked to be right, and especially so if challenged. This made me hard to work with.

In one dominant D trait, I expected people to do work right (according to what I thought was right), putting pressure on them on the basis that I had picked them to do the job because I knew they could do it best. In the other predominant C trait, I preferred to do the work myself because then I knew it would be done right—or at least what I thought was right.

I loved to make plans and work in a project environment, although, sometimes, my D trait of getting it done interfered not only with wanting to get it done but also with doing it right, a reflection of my C trait. When those two traits clashed, it could be confusing for those working with me. Whenever people were upset with me, then my lowest S traits would come into play and I would soften my behaviour by trying to get people to get along, including with me.

I had a difficult time working with anyone who had strong tendencies toward being reserved and people-oriented. I had an even more difficult time understanding and being able to work with people who were outgoing and people-oriented. I didn't know why at the time. I just knew that I didn't really like working with such people. I needed them and had to get along with them—as did they with me—but I just didn't know how it could work. I didn't know what the reasons were for my apprehension.

In evaluating my personality traits, using the DISC Model of Human Behaviour, I discovered I had certain strengths, as others had, and that we all had certain challenges in trying to understand each other's strengths. But, first, I had to know where I was coming from in order to know where I had to go to work with other talented people who were different from me but just as talented in their own way.

I truly believe that knowing all of this beforehand would have helped me, the members of my team and the organization. I have been so impressed with the revelations from the evaluation process, using the DISC model, that I encourage everyone to learn more about it by visiting: http://www.personalityinsights.com.

Lesson 11

Who Should Champion the Project?

How big or small the company or organization is will determine who will champion the project. It is more difficult for larger than for smaller organizations to address this question. For smaller businesses, there may be only one choice—the owner or the business manager—and this may be a good thing.

I was often contacted by my peers in human resources in other organizations and asked if I would share with them the secrets of why my work in workplace diversity was going so well, when they were struggling to get their project off the ground. Their questions were almost always the same:

- How did you get the support and resources you needed?

- How did you get the boss on board?

- How did you get the workers (or union) on board?

- How did you deal with backlash to creating change?

Although there are specific answers to each of these questions, the overarching response is, You have to have the right champion for the process.

When the process is about organizational change, this means that everyone working for the organization will be affected. Therefore, everyone has to be involved in one way or another, even if their involvement is as simple as being communicated with.

When a project involves complete organizational change, the champion has to be the most powerful person in the organization, or the owner if the business or company is small. If the chief executive officers or the owners don't buy into the process for workplace diversity and make it their priority, then the project will go nowhere.

With the right champion in place, the questions are answered in this way:

- How did you get the support and resources you needed?
  I got them from the chief executive officer because he/she asked me to get the job done.

- How did you get the boss on board?
  The executive was already on board and asked me
  to lead the project on their behalf.

- How did you get the workers (or union) on board?
  I met with them, along with the chief executive
  officer, and discussed all the anticipated issues. I
  also invited the president of the association to
  discuss the process, so that they could look at next
  steps before they happened. This allowed us to
  discuss issues and reach consensus before taking
  action.

- How did you deal with backlash to creating
  change?
  I did this one step at a time, with the chief
  executive officer communicating the
  anticipated objectives and expectations for
  support to move the organization forward.

If we go back to the smaller business with a single
owner/manager, then the answers are the same but
the focus is on the owner/manager to get things done
as the lead.

The Relationship

The relationship between the project manager and the
project champion has to be one of support for each
other. On a few occasions, I needed the chief to step in

and fix things. He did. Other times, he needed me to reassure him that we were still going in the right direction, especially if there was some backlash. I did.

Lesson 12

USING THE FORMAL PROJECT MANAGEMENT PROCESS

Our organization decided to use a formal project management approach to deal with the complexity of the workplace diversity project. Not being trained in the area of project management, senior management hired a consultant to manage the details of this process, which was an excellent investment in my opinion. However, at first, as do many who have never used the process, I found it to be excruciatingly detailed and tedious to develop. This being said, building a solid foundation resulted in a successful project.

A good project management consultant can be worth their weight in gold. Every time there was a need to change direction, or drop a proposal from the project, or initiate a new proposal, or where we failed to meet a deadline, the actions were defendable as a result of the formal project management process. It made me a passionate fan of the process. This is why I believe in it.

Charter

Developing the charter is a step-by-step process and it was an excruciatingly slow one to me because I thought these steps were obvious. I could not have been more wrong. The charter outlined the purpose, goals and objectives of the project, along with the critical success factors, strategy, interim and end products, scope, schedule, budget, constraints, planning assumptions, risk assessment, project organizational impacts, reporting relationships, project priority, sponsor responsibilities, completion criteria and the project charter approvals. Ultimately, these approvals were absolutely crucial for me as a project manager. The charter agreement between me, as project manager, and the executive was crucial for me in trying to figure out what was expected, what the timelines would be, what the risks were and what everyone would do to make sure I could get the job done.

The Reporting Assignment Matrix

The reporting assignment matrix, also known as the RAM, was the next tool introduced to me during this project. No matter what part of the project we started on, we always decided first who had to approve each stage of the work, including developing the proposal. The lower down the reporting level the faster the work got done. The higher up the reporting level the more likely there would be a delay. When challenged as to why there was a delay, I could usually point to an approval issue.

As an example, in order to include both the community and the organization in this management change process, we agreed to set up a steering committee comprising representatives from many interested groups. It was a twenty-one-person committee that met once a month. Members were advised about our proposals and would be given the opportunity to express their concerns or support for the proposal.

After each meeting, I would work with both their concerns or their support to adjust the proposal accordingly. I would then take the final product to the person with final approval for the work proposed and who was identified through RAM. The higher up the management level required for approval, the more time it took to get the work started.

Although I could get a proposal ready in two weeks and before the steering committee within the month, and then adjusted thereafter within a week, it sometimes took up to six weeks just to get the proposal in front of the executive member who was assigned final approval. Then, it was a guess about how long it would take them to look at the proposal. The demands and time constraints at this level are phenomenal.

Once approved, we moved the work along. But, if the executive expressed concerns, then it was back to the drawing board, although not necessarily back to the steering committee. Ultimately, the executive owned the project and it was their responsibility to make the final decisions.

In summary, whenever the chief or community or internal members wanted to know why the process was taking so long to accomplish, I could point to the reporting assignment matrix and simply say, "This is the reporting process and this is where the proposal stands."

The To-Do List and the Schedule

Every Monday morning, I would review the to-do list and the schedule to see what was expected to be accomplished in the coming week, by whom and who else would be impacted by the work either being completed or late. The items on those lists helped me to plan my week.

If the formal project management process, with all its details, is not chosen, then I recommend that an organization, or business owner, at least consult with a professional project management process consultant to determine what tools can be used to help guide them through the process.

Afterword

I would strongly advise that you at least investigate what others are already doing in the field of diversity work. I was always amazed about how many people in my world of policing kept trying to be different, or unique, or become the first to do new things. Many others have already been through this process, so you should learn from them. I am certain you may see the same thing in the world of business.

I would recommend that you attend conferences, workshops and speaker events where ideas are exchanged, weigh their value and fit against what you are doing, take what you need and discard the rest. I suggest that you read books on the subject to help you understand how you want to manage your project and then keep reading to be aware of what others are doing.

It is also important not to give up just because there are changes in the organization's priorities. As with many organizations, things change over time. Chiefs and CEOs come and go and, with every new chief of police, or executive, there were different priorities that they set for themselves to accomplish during their term as head of the organization.

This was true for the Ottawa Police Service. The intent of the census taken in 2005 was to repeat it every three years to validate the progress of our work in making the service more diverse. Unfortunately, as can happen with any organization, priorities changed and the census was not repeated until after November 2012.

Workplace diversity is about emotions as much as it is about connectivity and reflection. It has to feel right and be right. I never cared much for statistics about our success but I did like the pictures that those statistics demonstrated as a result of the diversity project. For a police service that thought it was not very diverse, the following is a snapshot of what we looked like three years into the project:

> Our members we[re] anywhere from 24 to 64 years old; single, married, common-law, separated and divorced: with children and not; handicapped; heterosexual, gay, lesbian, bisexual, two-spirited, questioning; ha[d] no religion, [or were] Buddhist, Christian Orthodox, Christian, Hindu, Jewish, Muslim, Protestant, Roman Catholic, Sikh and other; from the British Isles, French, Aboriginal – First Nations and Métis, North American, Latin/Central/S[outh] American, Caribbean, European,

African, Arab and Asian; and [had] everything from high school to [u]niversity degrees including 32 doctorates; and c[ould] speak in over 22 languages!

(This information was compiled from the census conducted by the Ottawa Police Service.)

It was a good start for us and would most likely be a good start for any organization as well.

Although there may be glitches along the way and the occasional moment when the project has to be set aside, as long as it is on the table for discussion or is part of senior management's business plan, it will always be acknowledged as an important and integral part in the growth of an organization. It is important not to give up just because there are changes in the organization's priorities and leadership. The end result will be well worth the effort of sticking to the project plan.

About the Author

A former police officer with over thirty years' experience with the Ottawa Police Service, Syd managed an international award-winning diversity change project, which received the 2007 International Association of Chiefs of Police Civil Rights Award. For ten years, he was the officer-in-charge of managing recruiting and training for the Ottawa Police Service.

Syd is passionate about managing change through diversity. He has learned through experience hard-earned tips and techniques to help organizations become more economically viable and gain a competitive edge. He can take diversity project managers from panicked to passionate to successful because he has walked the talk in an organization entrenched in 150 years of tradition.

In 2007, Syd was invested as a Member of the Order of Merit (M.O.M.) in policing by the then Governor General of Canada, Her Excellency Michaëlle Jean, for his work as an agent for change in policing in general and on diversity issues within a police environment.

Syd is also the author of *56 Seconds* and *How to Survive PTSD and Build Peer Support*. He is a speaker and facilitator for the development of resistance and resiliency to trauma within the workplace.

His work on diversity and diversity project management was a side bar to his work on trauma survival, which proved the value of diversity from the secondary dimensions, that is, the beauty of what we can't see in people!

Testimonials

"Syd always met the goals established by the organization and performed his work at all times with a high degree of professionalism and integrity. He became, and still is, a passionate spokesperson on the issue of diversity and achieving equity for all individuals within the workplace."

CHRISTINE ROY, DIRECTOR OF HUMAN RESOURCES,
OTTAWA POLICE SERVICE (2010)

"I have worked with Sylvio on several projects over the years and can attest that he is a competent communicator who always demonstrated a strong ability to analyze and solve problems. Sylvio stimulated us intellectually and challenged us to share ideas in search of creative alternatives. His work on problem-oriented policing, professional development and outreach recruitment were real-life examples of changes that contributed to the overall improvement of the police department. He demonstrated imaginative leadership and always inspired cooperation and confidence in others by respecting their opinions, their abilities and their contributions. He also possesses the ability to take appropriate action without offending people. Sylvio is committed to excellence and I wish him well in his future endeavours."

LEO JANVEAU, PROFESSOR AND STUDENT COORDINATOR,
LA CITÉ COLLÉGIALE

"As the Project Manager of Employer Training at the Toronto Region Immigrant Employment Council (TRIEC), I had the pleasure of working with Syd, whereby I contracted his services in 2010 for instructional design. Syd demonstrated his expertise in instructional design by taking TRIEC's existing workshop curriculum and turning it into a well-designed product by presenting it in a format that was appropriate for the fifteen or so Ontario college facilitators. On behalf of TRIEC, we were very pleased with the results and positive feedback from the facilitators. The redesign really helped me manage the project. Syd is a collaborative and forward thinker who uses best practices in instructional design to provide a high-quality product. Syd is easy to talk to, approachable and highly professional. He works hard to deliver his absolute best!"

NAV SINGH, MBA, CHRP (IN PROGRESS)

www.ingramcontent.com/pod-product-compliance
Lightning Source LLC
Chambersburg PA
CBHW071603200326
41519CB00021BB/6850